# GoAndPractice

## Fundamental Vocabulary for the Able Percussionist

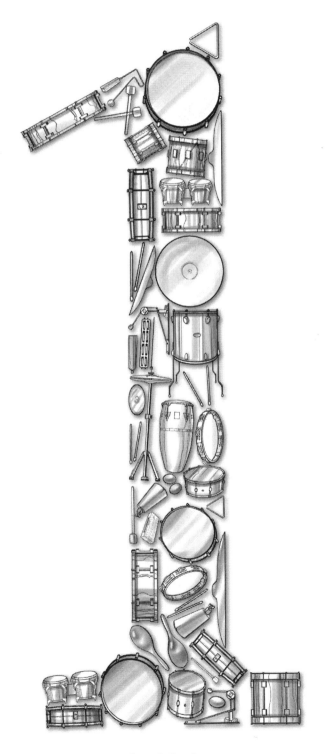

Alec Tackmann

*Special thanks to those who have helped in creating this book*

Michael King for creating the cover and interior artwork.
Karen Barrie for the design and layout.
Matt Meyer for the photography.
John Sievers and Marie Snyder for grammatical edits.
Judy Reishus for the presentation guidance.


*Also thanks to*
My longest-standing and most influential drum teachers Scott Ollhoff,
Rick Considine, and Terri Lyne Carrington.
Mark McKenzie for the years of invaluable career advice.
Berklee College of Music for an excellent four years of learning.
Humes & Berg Mfg. Co., Inc. for the support and top-notch drum cases.


*And of course*
Thanks to friends and family for the encouragement.
Thank you for choosing this book.

*Alec Tackmann*

ISBN 978-0-9861950-0-6

**$14.95**

# GoAndPractice® 1

## Table of Contents

Forward . . . . . . . . . . . . . . . . . . . . . . . . . . . . . 7

Technique . . . . . . . . . . . . . . . . . . . . . . . . . . . . 8

Introduction To Reading Music . . . . . . . . . . . . . . 10

Quarter Notes/Rests . . . . . . . . . . . . . . . . . . . . . 12

Quarter, Half, Dotted Half and Whole Notes . . . . . . . . . 13

Eighth Notes . . . . . . . . . . . . . . . . . . . . . . . . . 15

Whole and Half Rests . . . . . . . . . . . . . . . . . . . . 17

Dynamics . . . . . . . . . . . . . . . . . . . . . . . . . . . 17

Eighth Rests . . . . . . . . . . . . . . . . . . . . . . . . . 19

Dotted Quarter and Half Notes . . . . . . . . . . . . . . . 21

Sixteenth Notes . . . . . . . . . . . . . . . . . . . . . . . 23

Dynamics Part 2 . . . . . . . . . . . . . . . . . . . . . . . 24

Repeats . . . . . . . . . . . . . . . . . . . . . . . . . . . . 25

Sixteenth and Eighth Note Combinations . . . . . . . . . . . 27

Sixteenth Rests . . . . . . . . . . . . . . . . . . . . . . . . 29

Dotted Eighth Notes . . . . . . . . . . . . . . . . . . . . . 30

More Eighth/Sixteenth Combinations . . . . . . . . . . . . . 31

Accents . . . . . . . . . . . . . . . . . . . . . . . . . . . . 33

Flams . . . . . . . . . . . . . . . . . . . . . . . . . . . . . 34

Drags . . . . . . . . . . . . . . . . . . . . . . . . . . . . . 36

Five-Stroke Roll . . . . . . . . . . . . . . . . . . . . . . . 38

Nine-Stroke Roll . . . . . . . . . . . . . . . . . . . . . . . 40

Long Rolls . . . . . . . . . . . . . . . . . . . . . . . . . . . 42

Paradiddle . . . . . . . . . . . . . . . . . . . . . . . . . . . 44

Paradiddle Variations . . . . . . . . . . . . . . . . . . . . . 45

3/8 Time . . . . . . . . . . . . . . . . . . . . . . . . . . . . 46

6/8 Time . . . . . . . . . . . . . . . . . . . . . . . . . . . . 47

9/8 Time . . . . . . . . . . . . . . . . . . . . . . . . . . . . 48

12/8 Time . . . . . . . . . . . . . . . . . . . . . . . . . . . 49

Final Review . . . . . . . . . . . . . . . . . . . . . . . . . 50

Glossary . . . . . . . . . . . . . . . . . . . . . . . . . . . . 53

# Forward

This book is an introduction to the foundational elements of drumming. While the book is focused on the snare drum, its contents are applicable to many percussion instruments. It intentionally omits subjective matters regarding technique, reading, and musical expression; however, the "right hand lead" method is employed to create a standardized sticking pattern with the aim to increase hand/eye coordination. It is suggested that this book be treated as a backbone for the beginner and intermediate phases of learning while integrating style-specific material later as the student's musical interests become clearer.

Since this book is intended as a teaching aid, finding a *qualified* instructor is strongly recommended. A good teacher should potentially have a degree in music, professional performing experience, availability for regular sessions, and most importantly, a demeanor that will inspire the student to practice independently.

Throughout this book, counting and right/left hand suggestions are printed in gray when each new subject is presented. They are gradually removed to prevent the student from becoming dependent on them. When new topics are introduced, select vocabulary will be highlighted in bold print. Refer to the glossary in the back of this book if you need further explanation of the bolded terminology. It is strongly suggested that a metronome should be used when practicing and that the tempo is varied occasionally from one exercise to the next.

Alec Tackmann

# Technique

Holding the drumsticks with a healthy technique is very important in becoming a good player. Remember, *different techniques can be necessary for different playing situations.* While the rules below will apply for most general purposes, different grips will be used depending on what type of drum you are playing, what style of music you will be performing, or what your specific ensemble requires.

### Grip

- Place thumb on the side of the stick.
- The index finger will be slightly in front of the thumb.
- The middle finger will be slightly behind the thumb.
- Wrap the ring and pinky fingers around the base of the stick.
- Approximately one inch of the stick should remain beyond the pinky finger.
- Hold the stick loosely, but keep all fingers on the stick.

### Hand Positioning

- In most situations, the back of your hands should remain up.
- Be sure the tips of the sticks hit within approximately two inches of each other for tone consistency.
- Try to hold the sticks at a 90-degree angle.
- Your elbows may either stay relaxed or stick out.

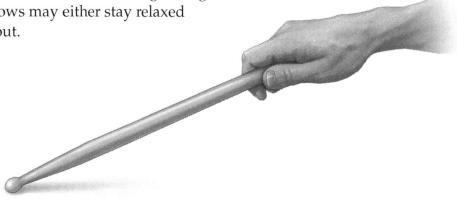

If you are doing all of this correctly, you should be able to see the butt end of the stick over the top of your wrist while the tips of the sticks are down:

**The Stroke**

The stroke will be generated from a mixture of finger and wrist movement.
Let the stick bounce back after hitting the drum using the stick's natural inertia.
For most situations, be sure to only make one **"tap"** sound; do not press the stick into the head.

**"Do Not's"**

Do not put your index finger on the top of the stick.
Do not stick out your pinky fingers, *especially during rolls.*
Do not make your index finger and thumb do all the work.
Do not let the stick fall into the crease of your palm.
Do not hold the sticks parallel to one another.
Do not bend your thumb forward.

# Introduction To Reading Music

Nearly all music has a constant **pulse** that a listener can feel. Typically, it is a percussionist's role in an ensemble or group to highlight that pulse.

The pulse of a song is often divided into cycles of four, three, or six **beats**. Each of these cycles is written into a **measure** and is contained within **bar lines**.

To identify how many beats will occur in each measure, a **time signature** is shown at the beginning of each piece of music. It usually includes two numbers on top of each other. The top number shows how many beats are in a measure. The bottom number shows which type of note is assigned to the pulse. To begin, a "4" will be used on the bottom, meaning a quarter (1/4) note will occupy each pulse.

**4** Four pulses per measure
**4** Quarter note is the pulse

**3** Three pulses per measure
**4** Quarter note is the pulse

A **rhythm** is a variation of the pulse played by the musician. It is made of long and/or short sounds and follows the pulse mathematically. Rhythms are represented on paper by music **notes**. Each note type is matched by a **rest** of equal value. While a rest occupies the same amount of time in a measure as its matching note, it will be silent. In music that has a four as the bottom number in the time signature, notes and rests have the following values:

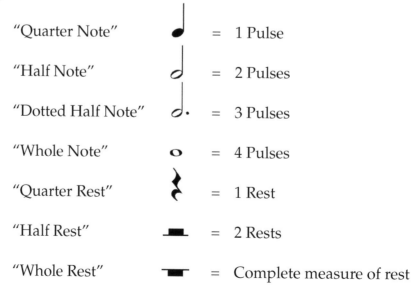

| | | |
|---|---|---|
| "Quarter Note" | ♩ | = 1 Pulse |
| "Half Note" | ♩ | = 2 Pulses |
| "Dotted Half Note" | ♩. | = 3 Pulses |
| "Whole Note" | o | = 4 Pulses |
| "Quarter Rest" | 𝄽 | = 1 Rest |
| "Half Rest" | ▬ | = 2 Rests |
| "Whole Rest" | ▬ | = Complete measure of rest |

All of this is composed on a piece of musical framework known as the **staff:**

Here is an example of four complete measures of rhythm on a staff:

Notice how each measure only contains a total of four pulses. The bar line does not receive a count.

At the start of each line, a **clef** will be displayed to signify how the staff lines will be read. A **percussion clef** ( ‖ ) indicates use of un-pitched percussion. A **double bar line** ( ‖ ) will mark the end of the music.

Here are examples of two separate lines of music complete with time signatures, clefs, notes, rests, bar lines, and double bar lines.

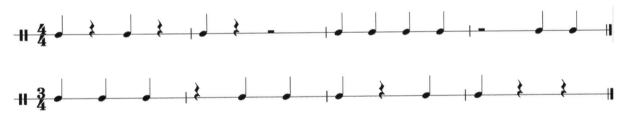

In percussion, a **sticking** will often be written beneath each note to indicate which hand should be used for that note. The right hand will be shown with "R" and the left hand will be shown with "L". In this book, numerical counting will also be written above selected measures of music.

Refer to the glossary in the back of this book if you need further explanation of bolded terminology.

# Quarter Notes/Rests

Remember: Both the quarter note ( ♩ ) and quarter rest ( 𝄽 ) receive one beat in time signatures that have a four as the bottom number.

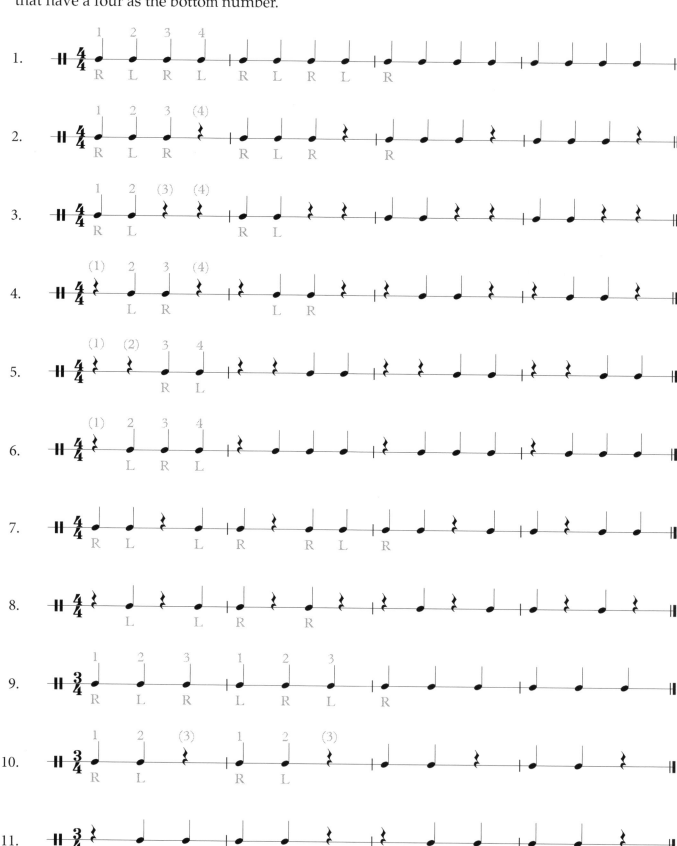

# Quarter, Half, Dotted Half and Whole Notes

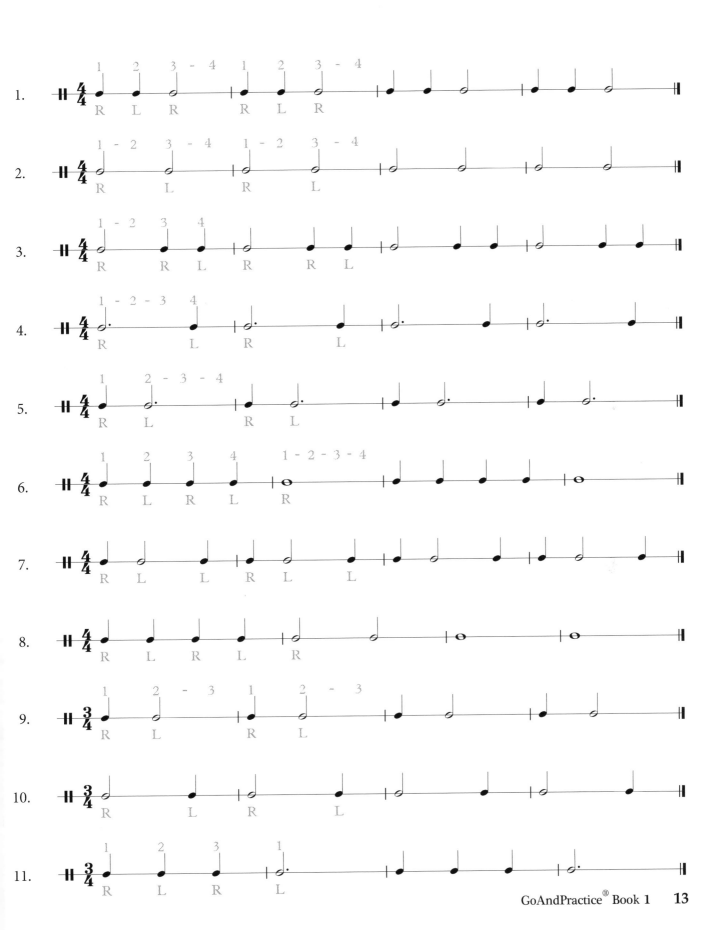

# Review

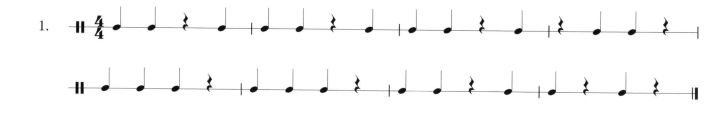

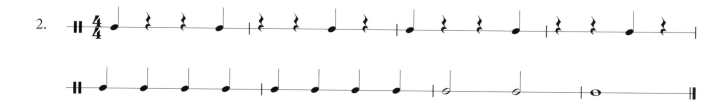

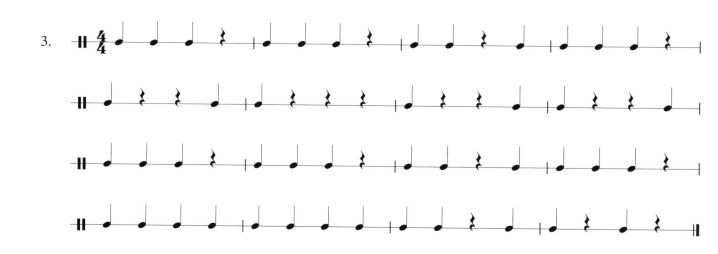

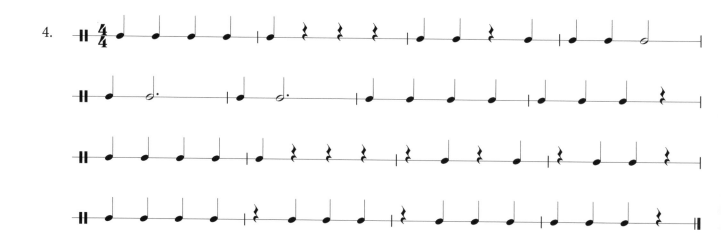

# Eighth Notes

An **eighth note** (1/8) is half the length of a quarter note (1/4), therefore counted twice as fast.
A lone eighth note will have a single beam hanging from its stem. Multiple eighth notes will have
a single beam connecting their stems.

Eighth notes are counted "ONE and TWO and THREE and FOUR and…" Notice how the numbers
still land on the pulse.

Groups of eighth notes are identified by a thickened single horizontal beam connecting the stems of the notes. It does not matter how many are grouped together.

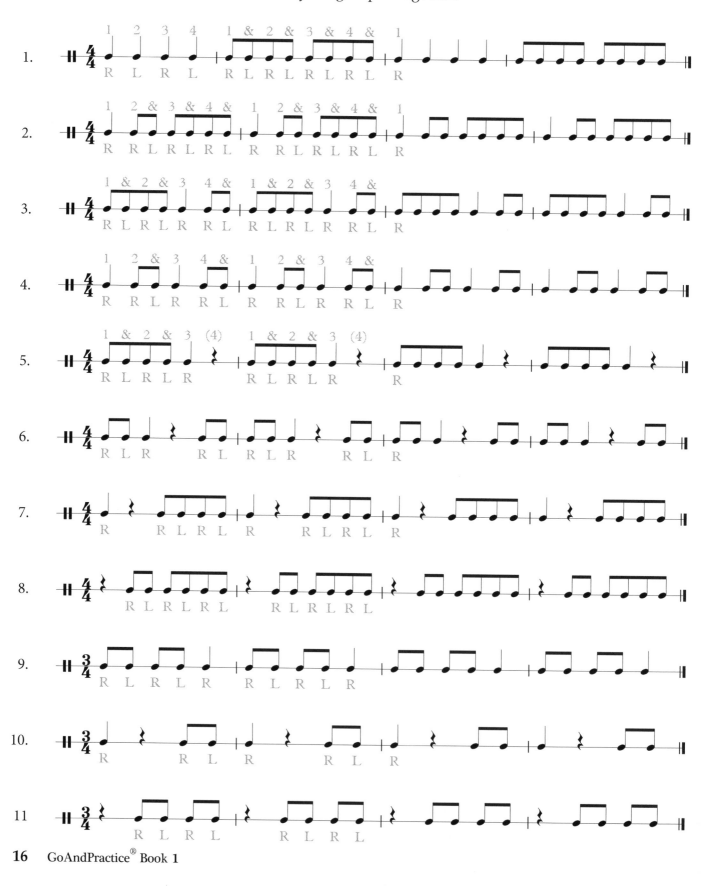

# Whole and Half Rests

Remember: A **half rest** will occupy two counts while a **whole rest** will consume an entire measure no matter what size it is.

## Dynamics

In music, **dynamics** are the application of softer or louder playing. Soft is represented by $p$ which stands for **piano**, the Italian word for gentle. Loud is represented by $f$ which stands for **forte**, the Italian word for strong. These symbols will be found underneath the staff. The player should stay in each dynamic range until noted otherwise.

# Review

1.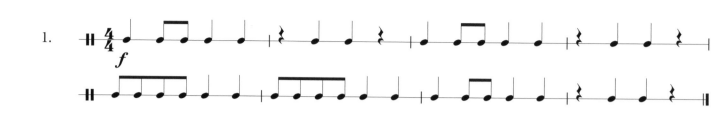

2.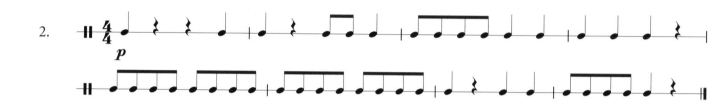

3.

4.

# Eighth Rests

As stated earlier, for each type of note there exists a rest of the same duration. An **eighth rest** is the same length as an eighth note. An eighth rest will also introduce the single eighth note.

$$ \eighthnote = \eighthrest $$

Notice the eighth note's single beam is now hanging in the form of a flag.

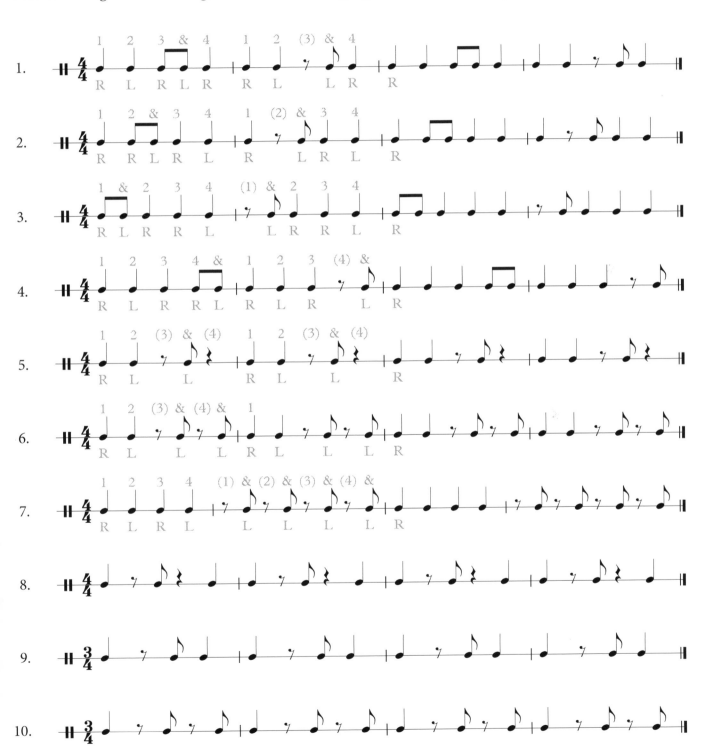

# Review

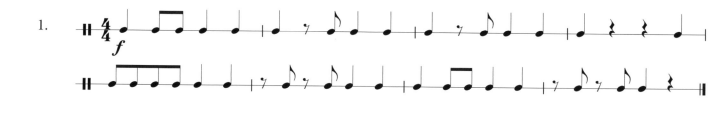

# Dotted Quarter and Half Notes

In musical notation, a **dot** following a note indicates that the note's duration will be increased by half of the original value. For example, as a normal quarter note is worth two eighth notes, a dotted quarter will be worth three eighth notes.

# Review

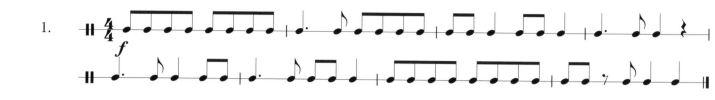

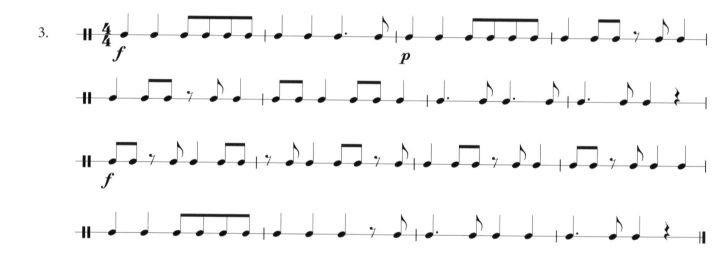

## Sixteenth Notes

A **sixteenth note** (1/16) is half the length of an eighth note making it twice as frequent. Groups of sixteenth notes are identified as having two horizontal beams touching their stem. Sixteenth notes in a sequence will be counted "ONE e and ah TWO e and ah THREE e and ah FOUR e and ah…". Notice how the numbers still align with the pulse.

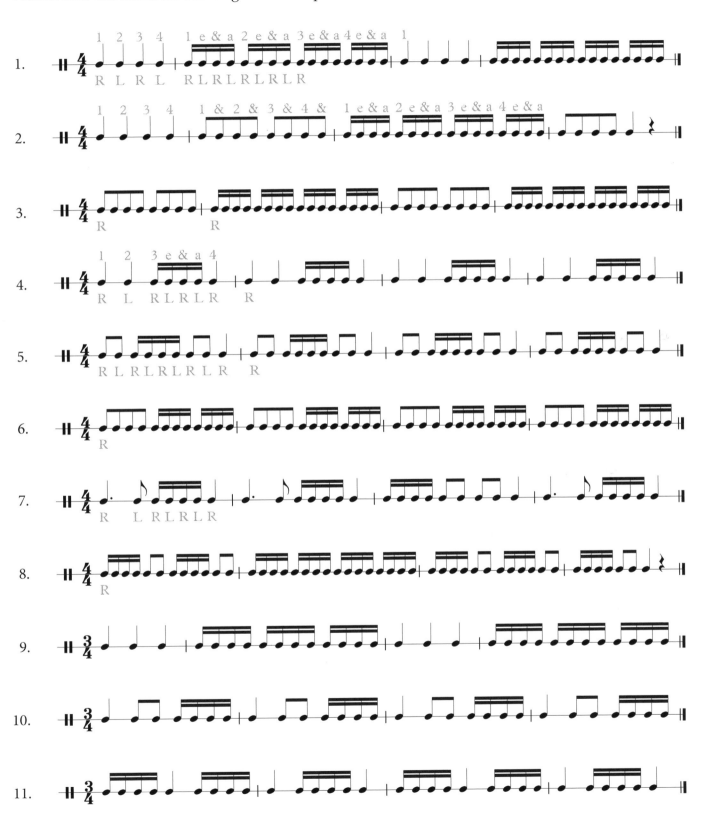

More dynamics exist than piano and forte. Inbetween the two lie **mezzo piano** ( *mp*) and **mezzo forte** ( *mf*) with "mezzo" meaning "half." To grow louder than forte is **fortissimo** ( *ff*) or **double forte** followed by **fortississimo** ( *fff*) or **triple forte**. Likewise, to grow softer than piano is **pianissimo** ( *pp*) or **double piano** followed by **pianississimo** (*ppp*) or **triple piano**. The complete scale of dynamics from soft to loud is as follows:

$$ppp \quad pp \quad p \quad mp \quad mf \quad f \quad ff \quad fff$$

There is no official volume measurement for each dynamic. It is up to the player's estimation; however, *each change in dynamic must be relative to the rest of the dynamics in the music.*

A gradual increase in volume is called a **crescendo** (*cresc.*) while a gradual decrease in volume is called a **decrescendo** (*decresc.*) or **diminuendo** (*dim.*). In music notation, they will either be written with their abbreviation, or they will be indicated with these symbols beneath the staff:

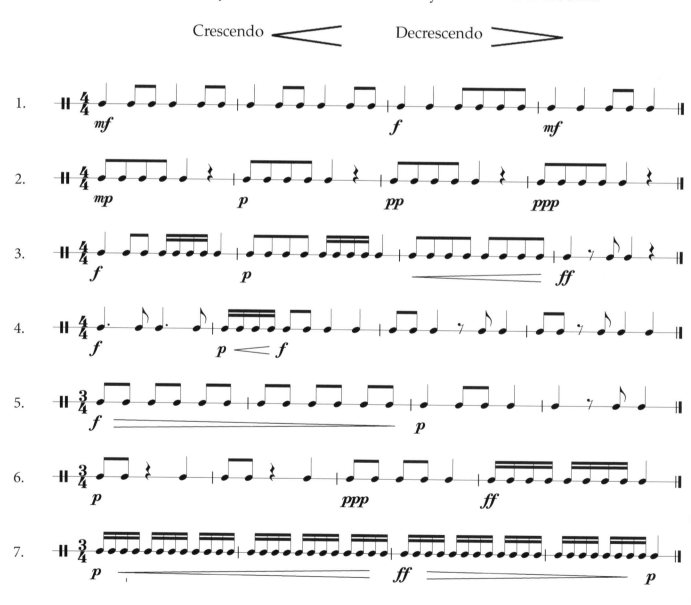

# Repeats

To save space on paper, arrangers will often write **repeats** in the music. These can happen in two ways: repeat signs and measure repeats. Repeat signs can occur anywhere in the music; however, they are usually found near the end of a musical phrase. They are identified as a double measure line with two dots:

Repeat signs direct the player either back to the beginning of the piece or to the previous forward facing repeat sign.

Measure repeats are used when a player has to repeat a specific pattern over the span of many measures. The symbol is a diagonal line with two dots and simply means to "repeat the previous measure." They can be placed back-to-back as many times as needed, and are used very often in percussion notation.

# Review

1.

2.

3.

4.

# Sixteenth and Eighth Note Combinations

Remember: A sixteenth note will have two bars touching its stem while an eighth note will have one bar touching its stem.

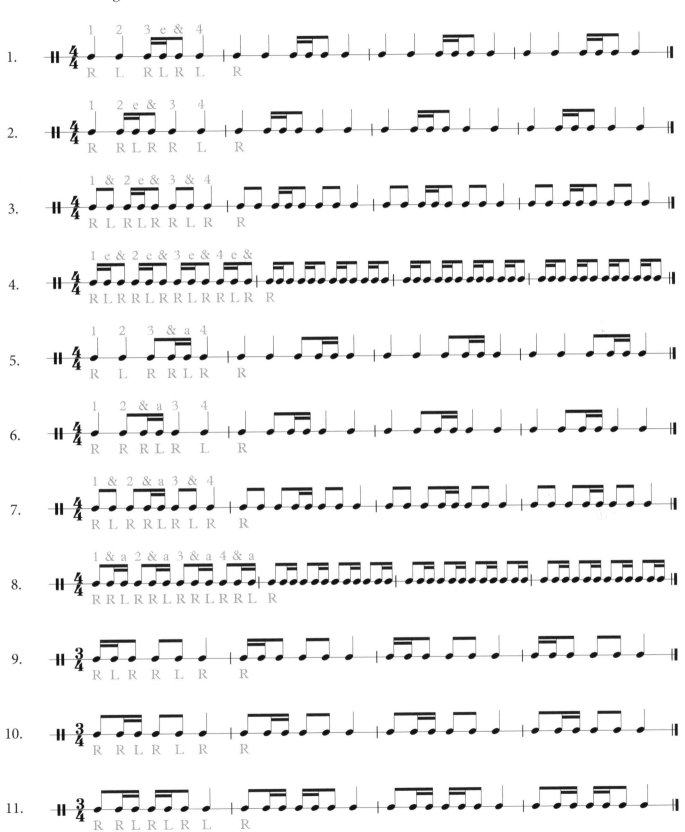

# Review

# Sixteenth Rests

A **sixteenth rest** occupies the same amount of space as a sixteenth note.

$$\text{♪} = \text{♹}$$

Notice the sixteenth note's double beam is now hanging in the form of two flags.

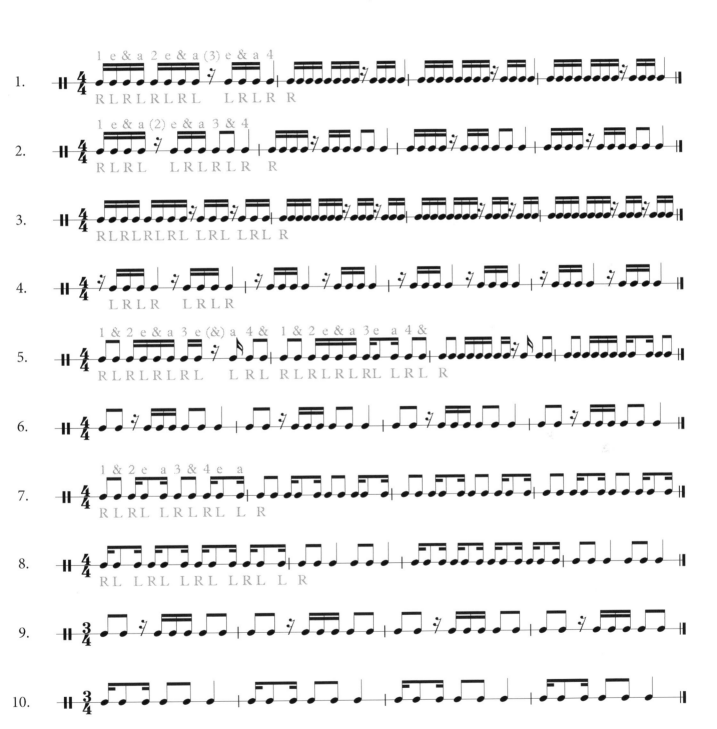

# Dotted Eighth Notes

As before, a dot will increase a note by one and a half of its original value. A **dotted eighth note** will be worth three sixteenth notes. Dotted eighth notes will introduce two common figures:

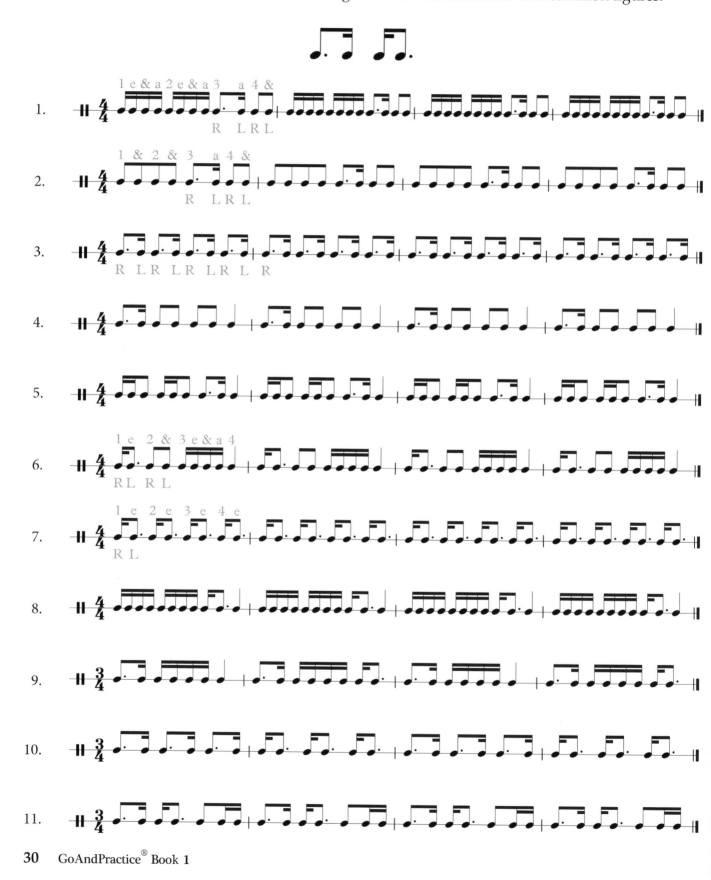

# More Eighth/Sixteenth Combinations

# Review

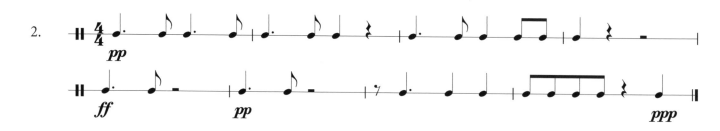

# Accents

An **accent** is an increase in a single note's volume. An accented note should be noticeably louder than a regular tap, and its actual volume should be relative to its context. It is signified by an accent ( > ) placed directly above the effected note.

To make an accented stroke, simply raise the stick higher and strike the drum slightly harder. Be sure to increase the volume of accented notes only without changing the volume of any surrounding unaccented notes.

# Flams

A **flam** is a regular tap stroke plus a **grace note**. In percussion, a grace note is a very soft note played by the opposite hand just before the original tap. The grace note does not receive a count; it is only for effect.

The distance between the two notes of the flam will vary depending on the playing situation; however, the strokes are not to be simultaneous.

There are two types of flams, a right flam and a left flam. In your music, they will look like this:

To play a right flam, strike the drum normally with your right hand and have the left play the grace note. To get the proper tone, prepare by raising your right hand normally while keeping your left hand lower than two inches off the drum. *In this situation, the right hand will receive the count, not the left.* A left flam is the same as the right flam but with left and right roles reversed.

# Flams Continued

1.

2.

3.

4.

5.

6.

7.

8.

9.

10.

11.

# Drags

**Drags** are similar to flams but have two grace notes. The same rules for the flam will apply to the drag; the grace notes must be small and not receive a count. A complete drag will have three strokes.

The grace notes will be executed with a **double stroke**. A double stroke is played by slightly loosening the grip, letting the stick bounce twice and catching the stick after the second bounce. It is important to retain proper stick grip in this motion. *Do not stick out the pinky or ring fingers as they are neccssary for catching the stick.*

Depending on the playing situation, the two grace notes can also be substituted for a single buzz stroke. A **buzz stroke** is made by lightly pinching the stick near the **fulcrum** and pressing the tip of the stick into the drum. The rebounds should be cut off at the tap stroke of the opposite hand.

# Review

# Five-Stroke Roll

A **five-stroke roll** is a **rudiment** made of two double strokes and one tap (2+2+1=5). It can be placed anywhere in music but is commonly stretched over the span of an eighth note.

The beginning of a roll will be indicated by a note with diagonal dash marks across its stem. The tie will point to where the roll must end. A number will often be placed above the tie indicating how many strokes must fill that space.

In this case, the five-stroke roll begins on the **downbeat** of the pulse and ends on the "and." Remember to end on a tap.

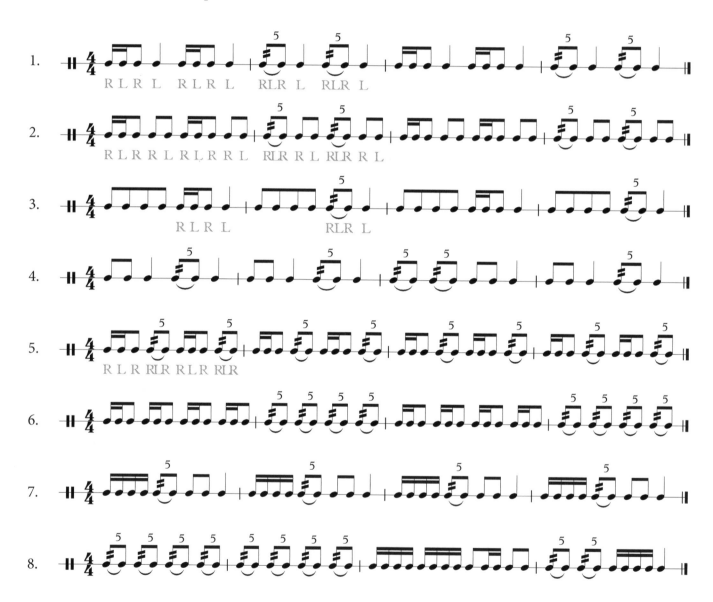

# Five-Stroke Roll Part 2

A five-stroke roll can also begin on the "&" of the beat and end on the following downbeat.

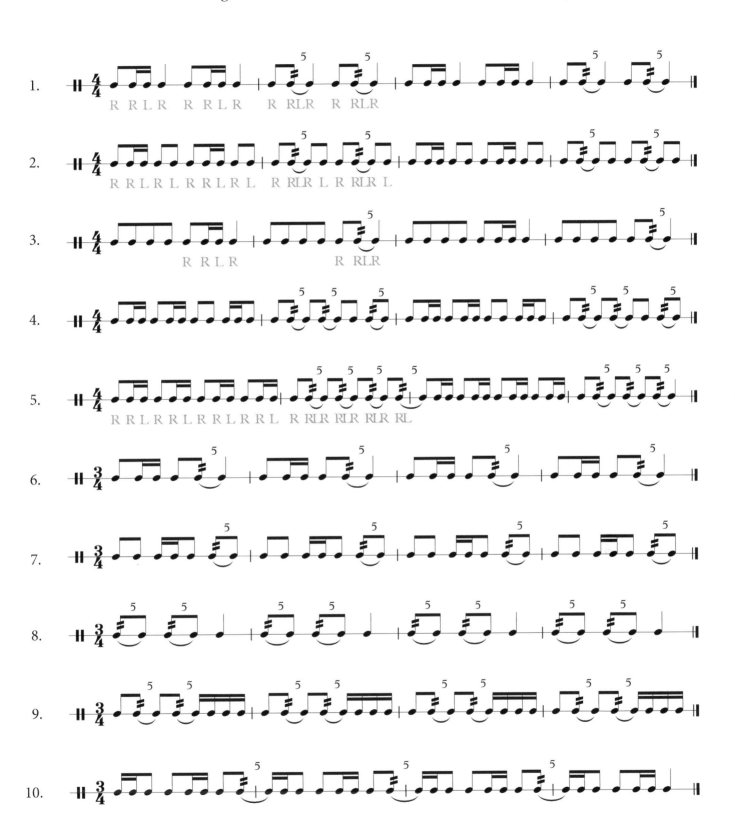

# Nine-Stroke Roll

A **nine-stroke roll** is a rudiment made of four double strokes and one tap (2+2+2+2+1=9). It can be placed anywhere in music but is commonly stretched over the span of a quarter note:

To play the proper type of roll, the player must know three things: where the roll begins, where it ends, and how many strokes fill the gap.

# Review

# Long Rolls

For rolls of longer duration, be sure to count the correct subdivision across each roll. Thus far, the rolls have been counted as doubled sixteenth notes.

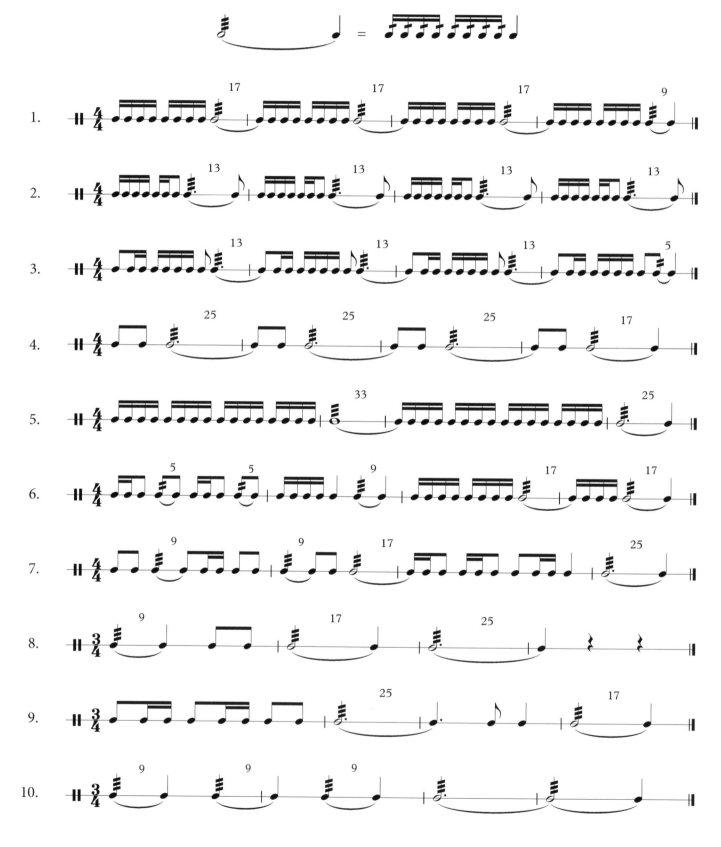

# Review

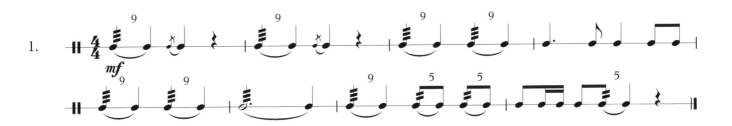

# Paradiddle

In percussion, a **paradiddle** is a sticking combination of mixed single and double strokes. The most common variation of the paradiddle is RLRR LRLL. It is generally applied as a device for navigating multi-surfaced percussion, utilizing the flow of double strokes, and for visual purposes.

# Paradiddle Variations

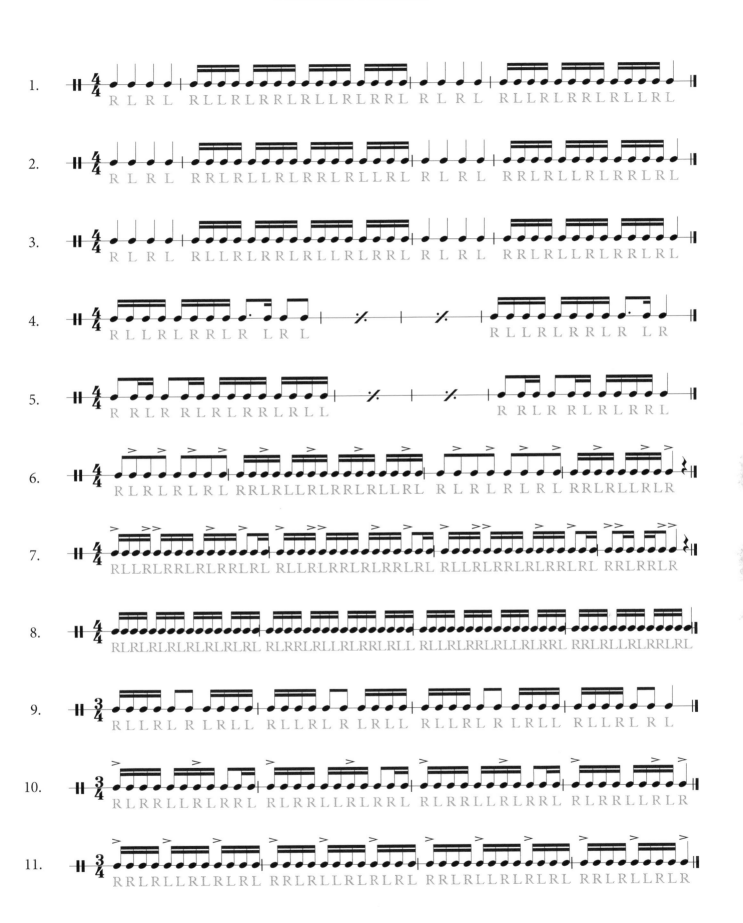

# 3/8 Time

In time signatures with an eight on the bottom, the eighth note will now receive a pulse. This will then shift every type of note so that it has twice the value it had in 4/4 time. For example, quarter notes are now worth two counts, eighth notes are now counted "One, two, three…," sixteenth notes are now counted "One, and, Two, and, Three, and…," and so on.

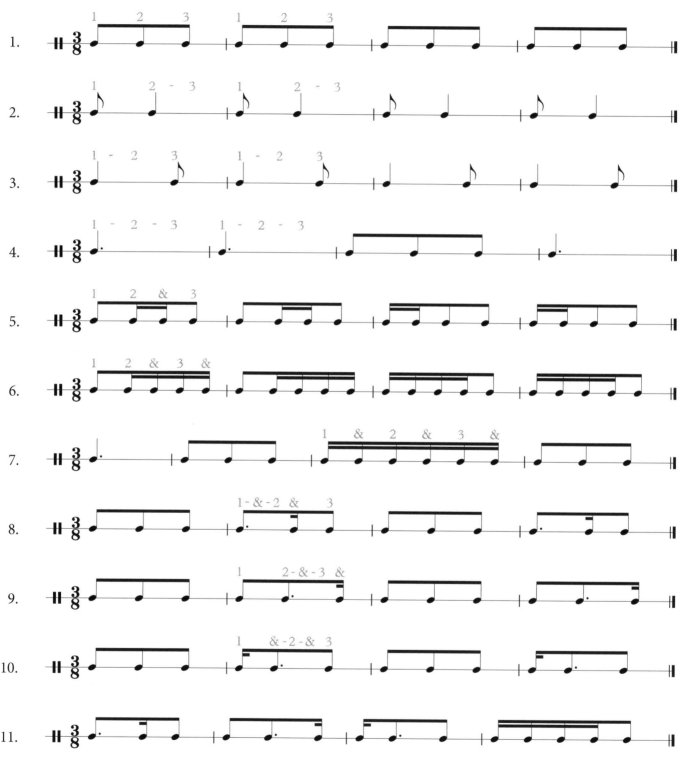

# 6/8 Time

6/8 time generally uses the same figures as 3/8 time due to the **imaginary bar line rule**. The pulse can be felt in "six", which is used in slower tempos, or in "two" (emphasis on beats one and four) for faster tempos.

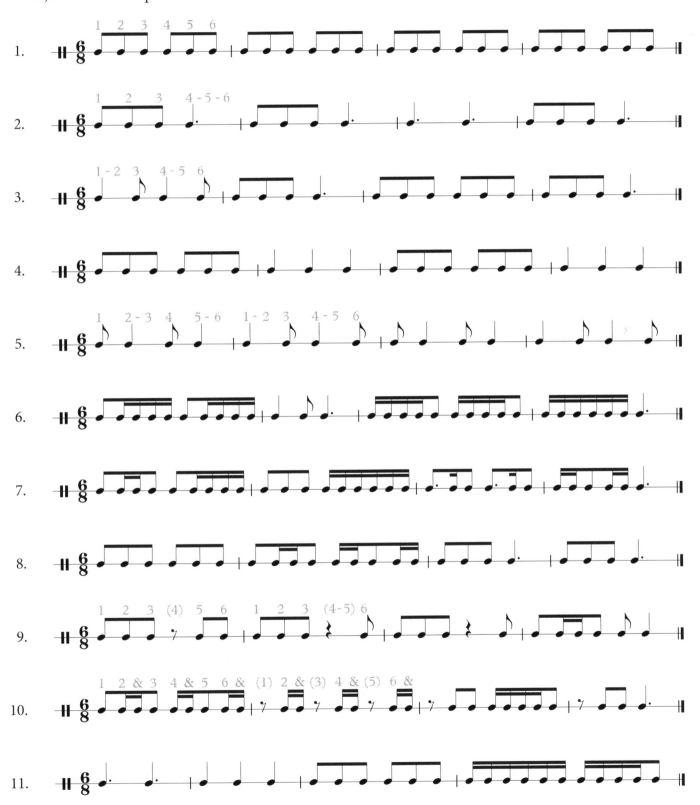

# 9/8 Time

9/8 time can be felt with a feeling of "nine" or a feeling of "three" (three groups of three with an emphasis on beats one, four, and seven).

## 12/8 Time

12/8 time can be felt with a feeling of "twelve" but is commonly used with a feeling of "four" (four groups of three with an emphasis on beats one, four, seven and ten).

# Final Review

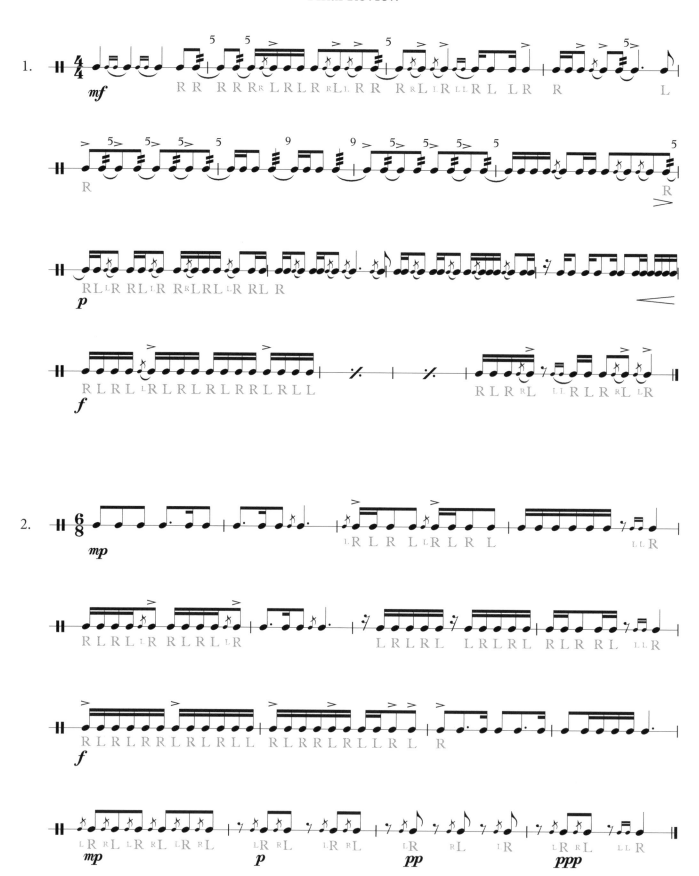

# Final Review

1.
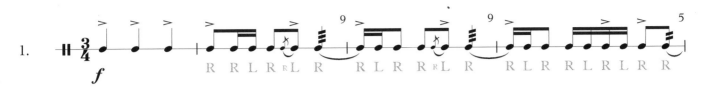

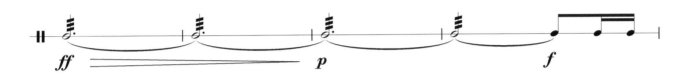

2.

# GLOSSARY

**Accent:** A distinct increase in volume of a single note.

**Bar Line:** A vertical line on the staff that divides music into separate measures.

**Beat:** A single emphasis in time. Multiple beats spaced evenly will create a pulse. Beats can be divided mathematically to create a rhythm.

**Buzz Stroke:** A drum stroke made by lightly pinching the stick at its fulcrum while pressing it into the drumhead. This will create a less defined "buzz" sound that is commonly used in snare drumming.

**Clef:** A symbol placed at the beginning of the staff to indicate how the lines of the staff will be read.

**Crescendo:** A gradual increase in volume.

**Diminuendo:** A gradual decrease in volume. Also called a "decrescendo."

**Dot:** Placed immediately after a note head, a dot will increase the note by one-and-a-half its original duration. The dot shouldn't be confused with a staccato dot, which is placed on top or underneath a note head.

**Double Bar Line:** The mark of the end of the music. It is made of one normal bar line plus one thickened bar line.

**Double Stroke:** In percussion, a double stroke is executed by letting the stick bounce beyond the initial tap and catching it again after its second stroke. Matching the volume of the second stroke to the first is controlled with the fingers.

**Downbeat:** The downbeat is the nickname of beat "one" in the music. The term can also be applied to beats two, three, four, and so on.

**Drag:** A rudiment consisting of two grace notes and one tap. The grace notes are executed by a double stroke or buzz stroke. Some texts will also call this a "ruff," where others identify ruffs as separate rudiments with the grace notes executed with alternating strokes.

**Dynamics:** In music, dynamics are the variation in volume of music.

**Eighth Note:** A note that is one-eighth the length of a whole note. Multiple eighth notes are counted "one and two and three and four and." Outside of North America they are called "quavers."

**Eighth Rest:** A rest that is one-eighth the length of a whole rest.

**Five-Stroke Roll:** A rudiment typically made of two double strokes and one tap (RRLLR)

**Flam:** A rudiment consisting of one grace note and one tap. The grace note receives no count.

**Forte:** In musical dynamics, forte means loud, literally translating as "strong."

**Fortissimo:** One level of dynamics increased from forte. Also called "double forte."

**Fortississimo:** One level of dynamics increased from fortissimo. Also called "triple forte."

**Fulcrum:** The pivot point of the drumstick between the stick and the thumb during a stroke.

**Grace Note:** In percussion, a grace note is a quieter note usually placed before a counted note for effect purposes.

**Half Note:** A note that is one-half the length of a whole note. Called "minim" outside of North America.

**Half Rest:** A rest that is one-half the length of a whole rest.

**Imaginary Bar Line Rule:** A rule in music notation where the downbeat of beat three must be visible in 4/4 time, dividing beats one and two from beats three and four. This helps the performer identify upbeats from downbeats.

**Measure:** A segment of music divided by bar lines. The size of the measure is determined by the piece's time signature.

**Mezzo Forte:** Translating as "half strong," a dynamic meaning moderately loud.

**Mezzo Piano:** Translating as "half gentle," a dynamic meaning moderately quiet.

**Nine-Stroke Roll:** A rudiment typically made of four double strokes and one tap (RRLLRRLLR).

**Note:** In percussion, a note is a marking on a staff that signifies a strike of the instrument.

**Paradiddle:** A rudiment made of combinations of single and double strokes, with the most common variation being RLRR LRLL repeated.

**Percussion Clef:** A clef that has no pitch assignment to its lines. It can be written with any number of lines and spaces depending on how many different surfaces are played on.

**Piano:** In musical dynamics forte means quiet, literally translating as "gentle."

**Pianissimo:** One level of dynamics decreased from piano. Also called "double piano."

**Pianississimo:** One level of dynamics decreased from pianissimo. Also called "triple piano."

**Pulse:** The repeating feeling of time. Can be felt at any rate, however it is usually consistent.

**Quarter Note:** A note that is one-fourth the length of a whole note. Called a "crotchet" outside of North America.

**Repeat:** Occurring near the end of a piece of music or a musical phrase, a repeat will tell the player to repeat the section from either the beginning or from the previous front facing repeat bar.

**Rest:** The silent counterpart to a note. For every type of note exists a rest of equal duration.

**Rhythm:** Variations of pulse. Constructed by notes and rests of different durations.

**Rudiment:** A piece of percussive vocabulary made up of combinations of right hand strokes and left hand strokes.

**Ruff:** See drag.

**Sixteenth Note:** A note that is one-sixteenth the length of a whole note in 4/4 time. Called a "semiquaver" outside of North America.

**Sixteenth Rest:** A rest that is one-sixteenth the length of a whole rest in 4/4 time.

**Staff:** The framework that music notation is written on consisting of single or multiple horizontal lines.

**Sticking:** The suggestion of whether to use the right or left hand for any particular note or group of notes.

**Subdivision:** The mathematical division of a note into smaller, equally sized notes.

**Tap:** A drum stroke that produces one sound.

**Tie:** A connection of two notes. Drawn with a curved line between the two notes.

**Time Signature:** The declaration of how the notes on a staff will be counted. Its top number indicates how many beats will occur in a measure. The bottom number indicates what type of note will receive a count.

**Upbeat:** A note occurring on the "and" of the beat. It is the opposite of a downbeat.

**Whole Note:** A note that is worth four counts in 4/4 time. It is known as a semibreve outside of North America.

**Whole Rest:** A rest that is worth four counts in 4/4 time and three counts in 3/4 time.

Made in the USA
Columbia, SC
14 September 2019